DEAR ANXIOUSNESS,

Can We Talk?

LOLITA E. WALKER
Illustrated by Brithany Disla

First Printing: 2023
Hardback ISBN: 978-1-7327928-6-9
Ebook ISBN: 978-1-7327928-7-6
Library of Congress Control Number: 2023907816

Published by Lolita E. Walker / Walker & Walker Enterprises, LLC.
16405 Livingston Road
Accokeek, MD. 20607
https://www.lolitawalker.com

Previous Works:
The Intersection of You & Change
Copyright © 2018 by Lolita E. Walker

Can We Talk? Letters & Poems to Reclaim a Bolder You
Copyright © 2022 by Lolita E. Walker

Ordering Information:

Special discounts are available on quantity purchases by corporations, associations, educators, and the general public.

For details, contact the publisher at the above-listed address.

U.S. trade bookstores and wholesalers: Please contact Walker & Walker Enterprises, LLC. Tel: (443) 353-9121 or email info@lolitawalker.com

WALKER & WALKER
E N T E R P R I S E S

2023

Dear Reader,
Can we talk?

THIS IS THE BOOK I WISH I HAD to have helped me discover and uncover pieces of me that sometimes seemed so hidden!

I remember many times when I felt anxious.

I remember my anxiousness leading to procrastination, my body balling up in what felt like a tight knot, and feeling paralyzed on what to do next. I even remember when that strange and complex emotion of anxiousness seemed to overtake my body, creating a wall of fear that prevented me from even wanting or trying to push forward.

Have you ever experienced this?

I also remember seeing my son, an elementary school scholar, who was becoming so worried and so anxious. He struggled to articulate what he felt inside, leading to even more frustration and anxiety.

Have you ever experienced this?

This book represents only one of the forty-four poems in my earlier book, *"Can We Talk? Letters & Poems to Reclaim a Bolder You."* My initial goal with this poem, *"Dear Anxiousness,"* was to gift my son a permission slip to talk about his inner feelings, which I wanted him to know were normal to experience.

Through my words, the illustrations of a 17-year-old artist, and soul-work that I have created especially for you, I pray that you are also offered a permission slip to talk to your *"Dear Anxiousness."* May it become a starting point for dialogue about what may sometimes still be hidden within you.

This book will empower you - and your inner critic too.

Dear Reader,
Can we talk?

This is to you, from me.
I love you,
Lolita

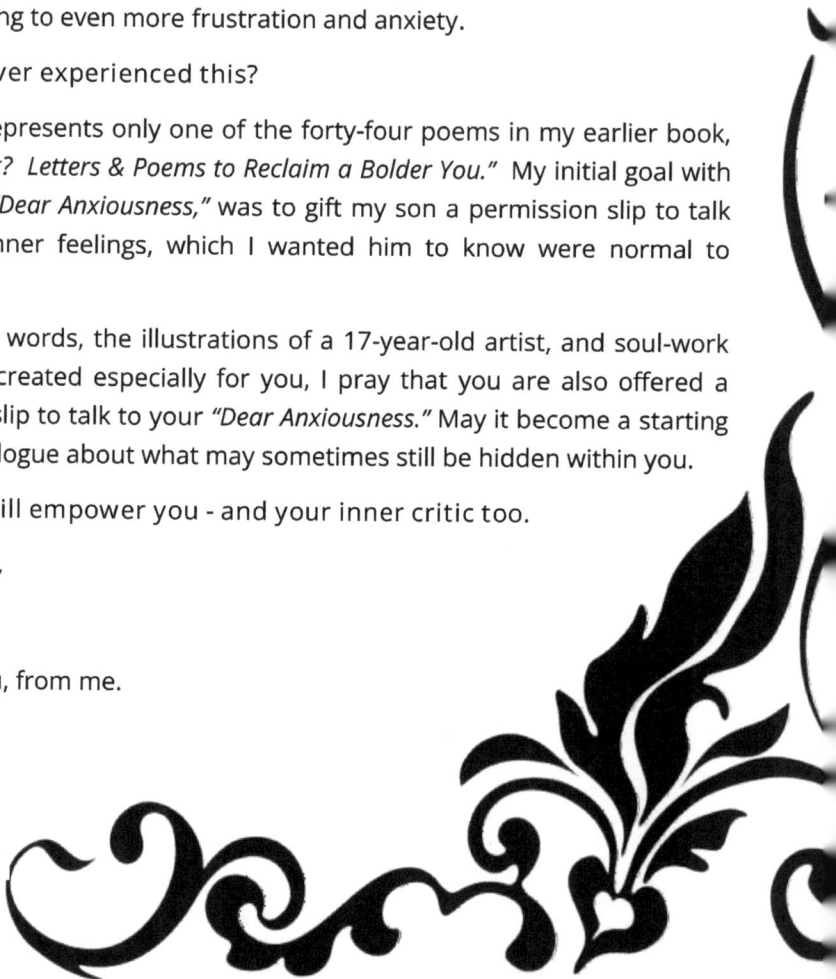

ANXIOUSNESS

[**angk**-sh*uh*s-nis, **ang**-]

---

noun

the state of being greatly worried; mental distress or uneasiness because of fear of danger or misfortune; anxiety: *The warm welcome from her new classmates made all her anxiousness go away.*

the state of being earnestly desirous; eagerness (followed by *to* or *for*): *As he sat in the cabin of the combat plane, he felt no fear or apprehension, just anxiousness to get airborne.*

---

https://www.dictionary.com/

THE DEDICATION

This book is dedicated to Brithany Disla, the 17-year-old illustrator, who brilliantly and creatively used her gifts to bring my vision and poetry to life!

Brithany, may any feelings of anxiousness that dare to come your way be covered by the greatness that you have gifted within this book, to an audience that spans the globe. May you always remember that your creativity has wings that will help you soar beyond where you stand today and where you believe limitations may exist. I am beyond proud of you. May this book serve as a reminder of the day you owned your "yes!"

To anyone who has ever experienced a level of anxiousness that has felt almost crippling, may these words penetrate you with the power to remember that you are uniquely made. May this book be the breath you need to regroup and show the world that you are here and that you are greatness! We need you!

THE CONTENTS

THE FOREWORD

Dr. Monica Goldson, Chief Executive Officer of Prince George's County Public Schools, Former Educator, Administrator, and Power Woman who creates new change daily.

Poetry has always been a powerful medium for expressing complex emotions and experiences that are difficult to put into words. In this poem, Lolita E. Walker delves into the depths of anxiousness and offers a profound and insightful exploration of this all-too-common experience. *"Dear Anxiousness"* captures a different aspect of the experience, from the sometimes-paralyzing fear and uncertainty to the restless thoughts and intense tension in the body to the overcoming and rediscovery of one's self. Through vivid imagery and language, Ms. Walker conveys the instinctive nature of anxiousness and its pervasive impact on our lives.

This book is a testament to the power of art, which gives voice to our innermost struggles and connects us with the universal human experience. This is only one of the books written by Ms. Walker in her must-read collection, *"Can We Talk?"* This book is for anyone who has ever struggled with anxiousness or knows someone who has. It offers a unique and compelling perspective on this complex and often misunderstood experience. It provides a sense of healing for those who have suffered in silence and a sense of empathy and understanding for those who seek to support them. This short book of poetry, illustration, and journaling is an essential read for anyone looking to overcome anxiousness and live a more peaceful and fulfilling life. I highly recommend this book to anyone seeking to better understand this complex and pervasive experience and find solace in art's beauty. Well done, Lolita E. Walker!

THE COMMITMENT

I've been told that my words have the power to stop anyone in their tracks and subsequently cause them to think deeply. Therefore, here's a warning.

***There will be times, while reading this book, you feel as if you are in an uncomfortable hot seat. Please know that this is normal and you are not alone. Consider these moments as reflections that have the power to unlock different pieces of you that were simply waiting to be unleashed.

May you give yourself permission to soar!

My Commitment to You

I, Lolita E. Walker, will journey with you through this book.

Your Commitment to You

I _____, (insert your name) on the date of _____, am committed to giving myself space to read, reflect, and feel the power within this pause. I commit to allowing these words to penetrate areas that may not yet be uncovered or unleashed within me. I commit to gifting myself all of me.

Signed: _____

Dear Anxiousness,

Can We Talk?

WALKER & WALKER
E N T E R P R I S E S

DEAR
ANXIOUSNESS

Dear Anxiousness,
Can we talk?

Last night I couldn't sleep.
I tossed and I turned,
as my heart pounded,
like the drums of my ancestors.

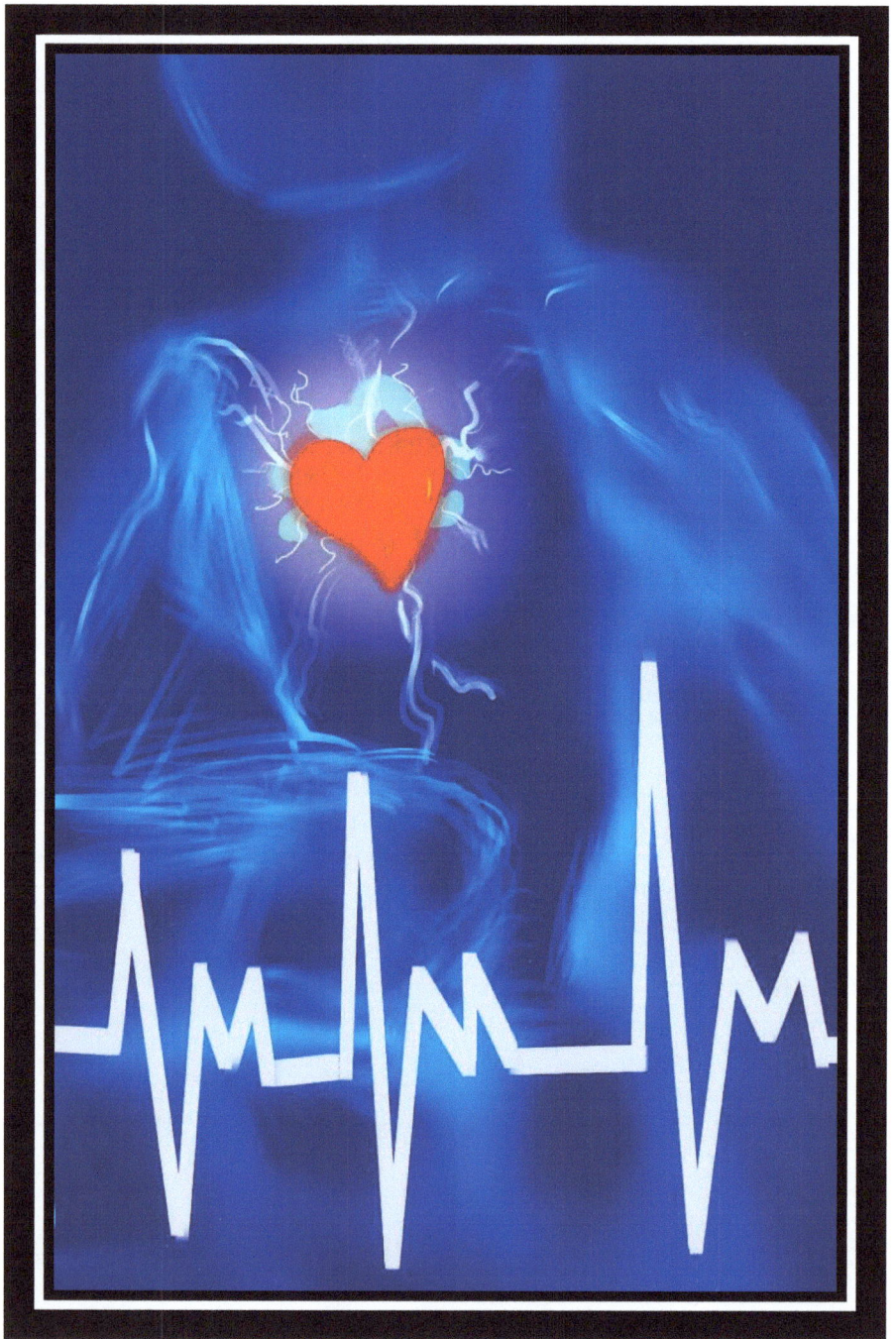

My blood raced.
It filled my veins
with the urgency
of now.

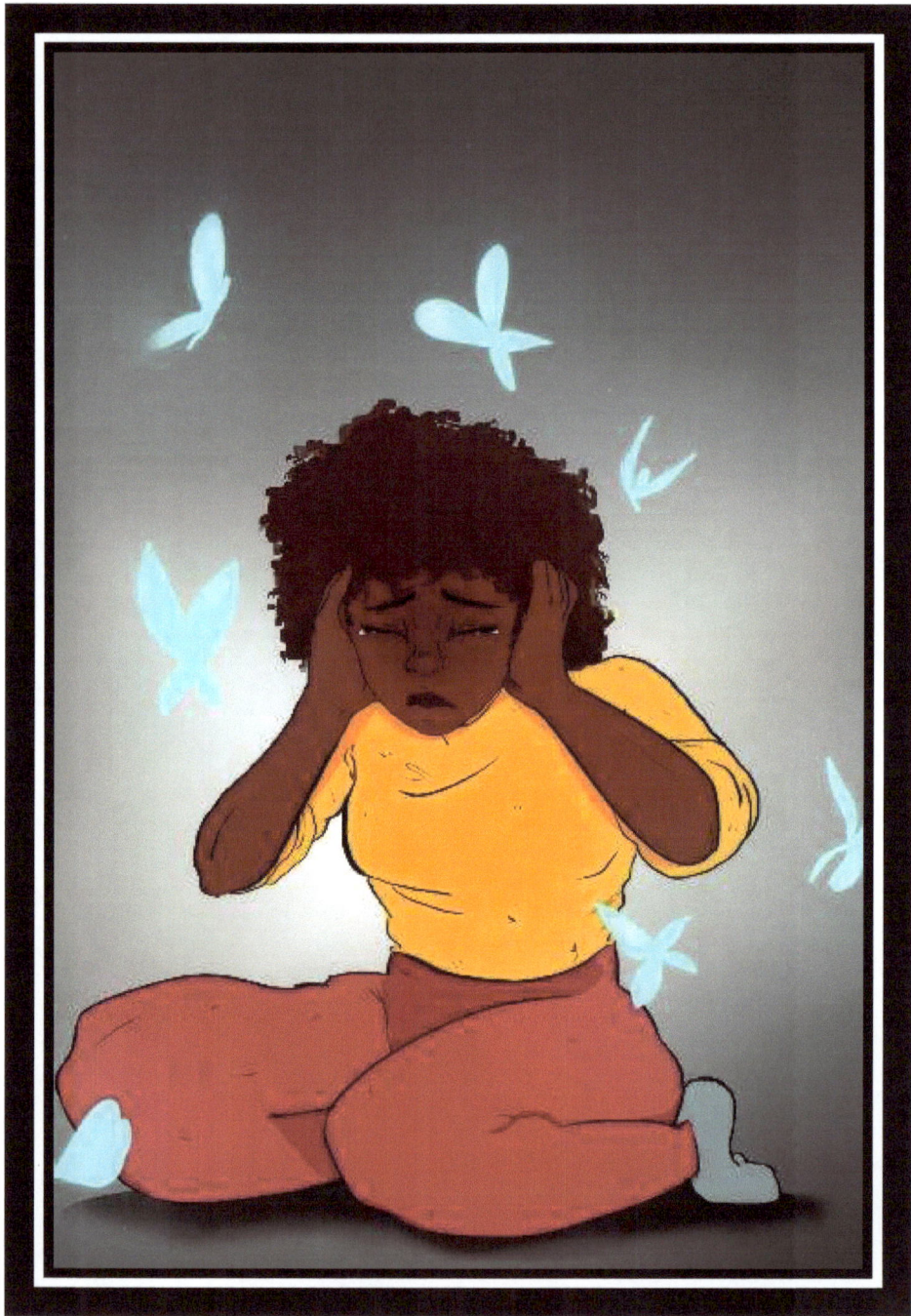

My mind fluttered.
I was fighting confusion
of what this war would and could be.

WOULD I **BUILD** A LEGACY?

My lips curled,
as I asked God to lead me on a plight
to fight
for freedom.
My freedom.

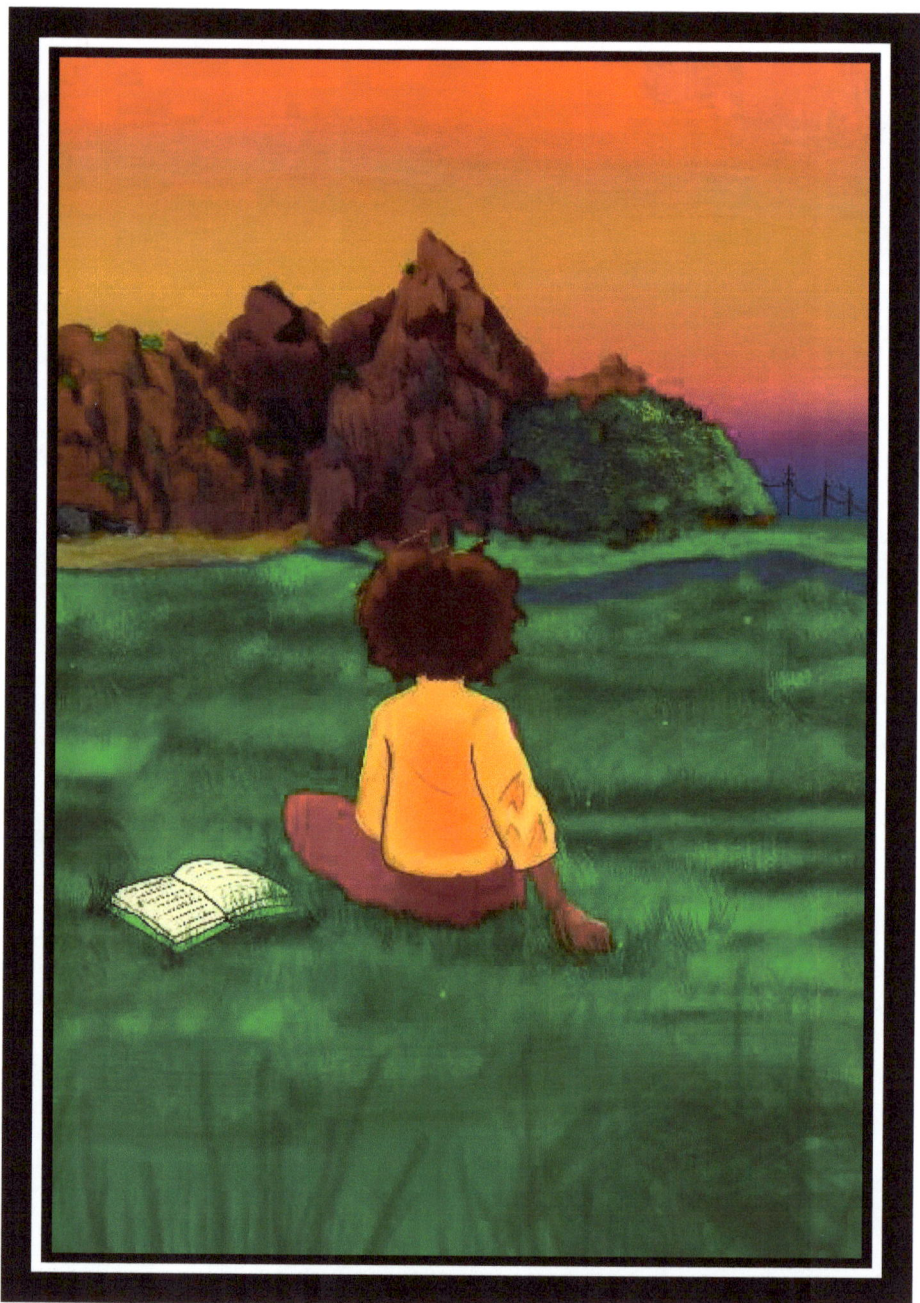

Will my freedom ring from the mountain tops?
or fall in the rivers that flow from east to west?
I ask myself if I am doing my best,
Dear Lord.

As the light from the sun shone through my window,
I hear the chanting of my tribe.
I feel the intensity of now,
realizing that I am ready.

CAN YOU SMELL THE
FREEDOM?

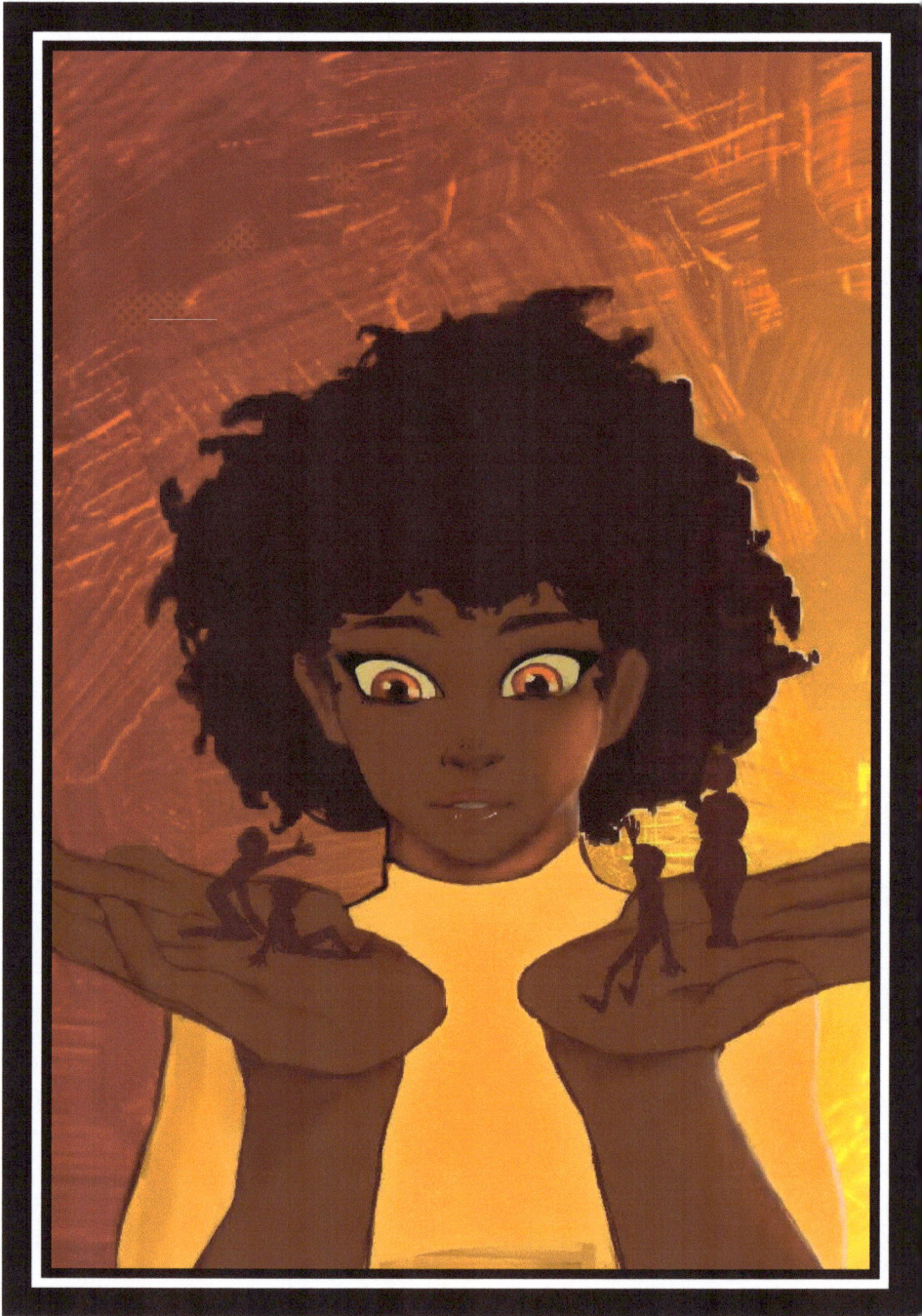

On the other side of your mind
is a tribe that stands for you.

There is a war of words,
thoughts,
energies,
of my mind.

I AM SEEKING TO FIND

ME.

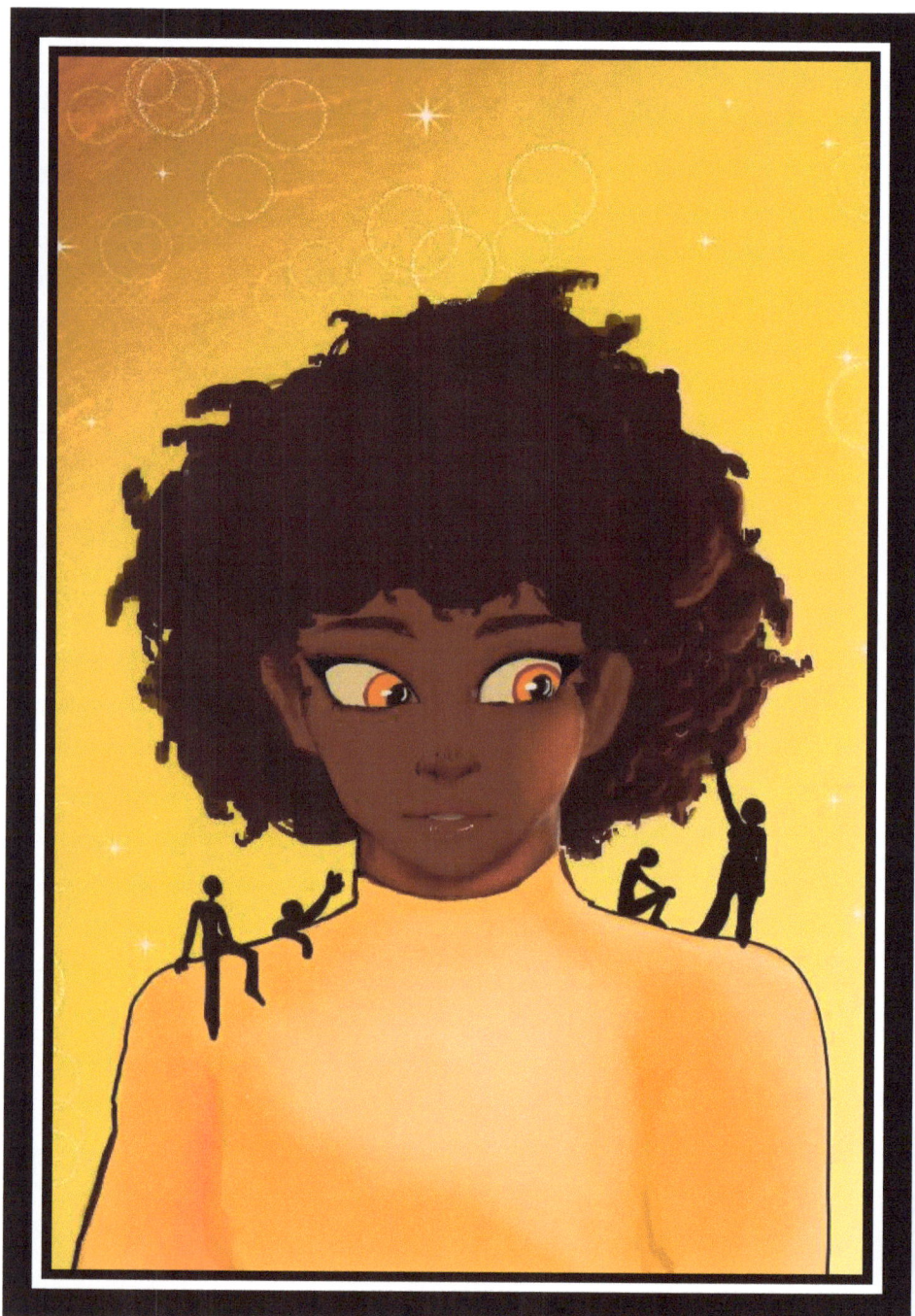

With an army by my side,
my intentions cannot hide,
my anxiety will subside
because my God is leading the way.

I CHECK MY INTENTIONS

AND

I

SMELL

Victory!

The history of yesterdays
and the stench of ignorant ways.

My senses are on high.

I now hear the birds sing with increasingly wild cries.
I feel the girth from the earth.

CAN YOU FEEL IT?

My birthright
has begun to rise inside of me.
I see the fire from across the land,
where we will celebrate the seven signs of completion.

I touch my neighbor
with the principle of Ephesians,
the unity of these bodies
fighting as one.

I
SMELL
Victory!

Close your eyes and breathe.
You are standing right here.

So, Dear Anxiousness,
Can we talk?

This is to you, from me.
I love you,

(Insert Your Name)

TAKE A MOMENT
TO TAKE THREE DEEP BREATHS.

SOUL WORK

When you feel ready, the next few pages offer a dedicated space for you to journal.

I encourage you to explore what is in your thoughts and on your mind. Some readers may feel a bit shaken, some may find joy and comfort within the words, others may choose to read and reread the poem to better receive the words, take in the imagery, and experience self-discovery. Even for me, every time I read this poem, my mind drifts to take control of my own *"Dear Anxiousness."*

Why journal?

Journaling has been proven to help release the feelings and emotions within you. It can be a great tool to improve your mental health, develop yourself personally, and reflect upon what is happening in your school, work, home, or life.

Journaling has also been known to be one of the many ways to help manage stress and grow personally and professionally. To think more clearly, increase self-confidence, enhance self-awareness, improve your capacity to solve problems, and consider alternative viewpoints, are all documented outcomes of journaling.

Here's your opportunity to engage in a bit of soul work, via journaling.

1. At this moment, after reading the book and experiencing my own *"Dear Anxiousness,"* I feel ...

_____

_____

_____

_____

_____

_____

_____

_____

2. I remember a time when I felt anxious about ...

_____

_____

_____

_____

3. When I really think about it, the 3 things that caused me to feel these emotions in the instance I noted within question #2 were...

1. _____
2. _____
3. _____

4. **If I choose only one of the three areas in question #3 to focus on at this moment, I would choose # _____.**

5. **I chose this specific focus area in question #4 because...**

_____

_____

_____

_____

_____

_____

_____

6. **If I were to now feel these same emotions, I would choose to ...**

_____

_____

_____

_____

_____

_____

_____

_____

7. The stanza of *"Dear Anxiousness"* that resonated with me the most was ...

_____

_____

_____

_____

_____

8. The reason that the stanza I noted in question #7 stood out to me the most was because...

_____

_____

_____

_____

9. The illustration within the poem that resonated with me the most was ...

_____

_____

_____

_____

10. The reason that the illustration I noted in question #9 resonated with me the most was because ...

_____

_____

_____

_____

11. **If I were to picture my *"Dear Anxiousness,"* I would describe it as ... (describe its look, height, weight, color, shape, voice, etc.)**

_____

_____

_____

_____

_____

_____

12. **If I were to write a letter to my *"Dear Anxiousness,"* it would say,**

Dear Anxiousness, _____

_____

_____

_____

_____

_____

_____

_____

_____

_____

_____

_____

_____

_____

_____

_____

_____

_____

_____

13. When I choose to take control of my *"Dear Anxiousness,"* I will feel...

_____

_____

_____

_____

14. When I choose to walk away from my *"Dear Anxiousness,"* I realize that it looks different. Now that I have completed my soul-work and have looked back at my earlier description that I noted in question # 11, I would describe my *"Dear Anxiousness"* as ... (describe its look, height, weight, color, shape, voice, etc.)

_____

_____

_____

_____

_____

_____

COLORING PAGE

Whether young or more seasoned, may you, in your quiet moments, enjoy a space to color a sketch by Illustrator, Brithany Disla.

May this be a space for you to color outside of your lines and express yourself freely.

THE ENDING

Whether for inspiration, motivation, or reassessment, I pray that my words and soul work, coupled with Brithany's illustrations were able to meet you where you stood, helped you to pause for a bit, and assisted you in unlocking the *"Dear Anxiousness"* within you.

I invite you to visit https://www.lolitawalker.com to stay updated on new books to the *"Can We Talk"* series, services, and products that can help to lift you higher. Please always remember that you are the greatness that others may have yet to see.

Remember to see the greatness in yourself. I do!

Also, please remember to check out my podcast, *"Coaching, Cocktails & Conversations"* on all streaming platforms and directly at https://podcast.lolitawalker.com . I cannot wait to read your 5-star review. Enjoy.

Thank you for trusting me on your journey.

Lolita

THE AUTHOR

Lolita E. Walker is a sought-after thought-leader, ICF professional certified life, leadership, and executive coach and keynote speaker at the forefront of a movement that empowers busy women and high-powered organizations to feel and trust the power in their pause, reduce overwhelm, and move distractions to achieve un-deniable results, NOW. After leading in the corporate space for nearly twenty years, Lolita founded her personal and professional coaching and consultancy, Walker & Walker Enterprises –

https://www.lolitawalker.com

A mommy of one son, Lolita's superpower is that she up-levels you through "spoken word gospel" to your mental, with the uncanny ability to pull the leadership and greatness that is hidden within. She is a business owner, author of *"The Intersection of You & Change"* and *"Can We Talk? Letters & Poems to Reclaim a Bolder You,"* podcast host of *"Coaching, Cocktails & Conversations,"* an all-inclusive, corporate and women's retreat cultivator, and change champion for YOU. Courses, 1:1 and group coaching, personalized affirmations, apparel, and positive products, are only some of the complements to her public speaking and coaching practice.

Lolita graduated from Morgan State University as an Industrial Engineer and Simmons College as a Master's in Business Administration. She is a Ph.D. student, an educator at Morgan State University, an active member of Alpha Kappa Alpha Sorority, Incorporated, is an elected official, and holds leadership positions in several organizations. She's been where you are and has gotten where you seek to be, in a renewed state of being. The benefit of having a partner who has reached the finish line successfully and systematically, is knowing that her methodologies are the enablers to help you and your teams soar beyond where they stand today.

Can we talk? https://www.lolitawalker.com

A REFLECTION FROM THE ILLUSTRATOR

Looking at my artwork, I see a reflection of what was once murky waters that flourished into blooming flowers. This is the acknowledgment that one doesn't always have to stay in the rain. Instead, they can find comfort and safety under an umbrella called love.

Each piece of art within this book has multiple considerations for how it could be interpreted. Most of the drawings hold warm, vibrant colors to encourage the overcoming of anxiety and the embracing of happiness and tranquility. As I drew each image, I experienced healing for myself and for everyone in the same situation of anxiousness.

The girl in this book has a story.
I have a story.
You have a story.

We are meant to express these stories and come together to speak about them.

Though there is only a singular girl that is drawn throughout the book, she is never truly alone. God, hope, and the world surrounds her, holding her up when she is at her lowest.

Lastly, as I reflect...

Having a surreal experience like this one is unbeatable as a first job. I will never forget it. I always worried that I would be haunted by all of the chances I didn't take. However, this is the one I took, and I will never regret it. Working with Lolita allowed me to try things that I had never done before. I'd never created digital art like this. It opened my eyes to a completely new horizon of opportunities for my future. I learned immensely, and thanks to Lolita, I have begun my journey to becoming a young, upcoming illustrator. To everyone who has read this book: never ignore an opportunity made for you. You may never see it again!

Keep chasing your dreams and let your anxiousness wash away.

-Brithany Disla

BEHIND THE BOOK

It started on a voice-only social app. I remember scrolling through the app and hearing amazing and powerful voices of poetry. I remember listening and thinking, WOW, I miss writing poetry. It had been years. I found myself yearning to hear more and impressed by the spoken word and creativity from each of the poets that came into the space.

I'd never referred to myself as a poet.

I remember one morning, about 2:00am, I logged on to the app and through the kaleidoscope of butterflies that seemed to wrestle in my belly, I read my poem, *"Dear Black Girl."* I took a deep breath and read it aloud to almost 250 strangers. I was pleasantly overwhelmed at the response. I began writing to picture prompts, to the emotions I felt when others were speaking, and even as a participant in poetry competitions.

I was surprised at myself!

I'd won second place in a poetry slam!!!!
I then took a poetry class to challenge my thinking and to learn about different writing techniques. The next thing you know....

I had written 44 poems!
I published them!
And I created an audiobook because people commented that they loved to hear the emphasis and power of me speaking my words aloud.

WOW!

As I began to read my poetry more and more, a former educator said to me, 'You should really get this into the hands of the schools.' She said, "Our young people really need this!" We began creating educational assessments to accompany my work; however, my book of poetry was denied by the first school system I approached. On the very voice-only, social app where I began, I asked if there was anyone who knew how I could gain access to a high school English class to host a focus group and discussion. I received a note from **Mindy Staley**. In two weeks, I was speaking with an English teacher, **Judy Sies,** from Whitehall-Yearling High School in Ohio, to lock in a virtual date. She had each of her students create a poster of inspiration from their favorite stanza of *"Dear Anxiousness."* Brithany, the illustrator of this book, was a student in the voluntary class.

Interestingly enough, when she walked into the room, I knew that there was something special about Brithany.

She walked in with a cute, oversized sweater and a welcoming smile, and sat directly in the front row. As I sorted through the posters, one of them stuck out as a great potential for the cover of my book. I immediately asked who created this amazing piece of art. When Brithany raised her hand, I wasn't surprised. I asked if she would consider becoming the illustrator for the first book in my new series. What she didn't know at the time was that I'd committed to creating a pictorial collection from several individual poems that were within my book, *"Can We Talk? Letters & Poems to Reclaim a Bolder You."*

This book, *"Dear Anxiousness, Can We Talk?"* is the first to be published in the series and I am so proud to have had the opportunity to hire a 17-year-old superstar.

This book is one of many to come in a series of pictorial poetry that talks to the inner you.

Please visit https://www.lolitawalker.com for the links to purchase additional books in the series and download the audiobook.

THE ACKNOWLEDGEMENTS

To my Heavenly Father and the Lord of my life, *Jesus Christ*. My strength, my encouragement, my light when darkness threatens to cloud my mind, and my compass when I lose my way on my path forward. Your presence, direction, and unconditional love are deeply and humbly appreciated and revered. Thank you.

To Brithany, the young illustrator of this book, who simply said "yes," may you continue to allow your gifts to help you soar. I pray for increased abundance and publications for years to come. To my son, *Walker*, who, at the age of 11, continues to motivate me daily, you remain the epitome of strength, encouragement, energy, love, & living fearlessly free. You push me beyond my boundaries with the simplest of questions and then tap into a youth that I sometimes forget resides within me. To my mommy, *Evelyn*, who provides me with support to further my dreams, you are a much-appreciated footstool on my entrepreneurial journey, an arm, and shoulder (literally) when I stumble and fall, and a resilient guide on my motherhood journey. I pray for increased love, happiness, and fulfillment all the days of your life. To my brother, *James-Douglas (JD)*, a calming voice through miles of separation, a positive reasoner in any situation, and an encouraging motivator. You are a stronghold of unwavering faith. I am blessed to have been paired with you for my sibling love. I am so very proud of you for so many reasons. Thank you for simply being you. To Dr. Goldson, who said yes to penning the foreword of this book, your inspiration, motivation, drive, transparency, and "get it done" attitude pushes me daily. You are a shining example of someone who I am so proud to follow. Thank you for trusting me and my work to power the inner strength of our young people. I am so grateful that God aligned our paths. Thank you. Stacy Luckett, thanks for pushing me to get this book into the hands of our youth and within schools. It was your push that spawned me to leap further and farther. To Mindy Staley, of Whitehall-Yearling High School, thank you for introducing me to Ms. Judy Sies, the English teacher who exceeded my expectations of a high school focus group, to have her students create posters, one of which powered this book. You are both magnificent examples of educators who shine a light on our scholars. You are conduits to help pull greatness from within. Thank you. Teachers are the magical gateway between what is in our minds and what can become our futures. You've ignited something special within Brithany and I pray that you always remember that you were two of the catalysts of her growth.

Finally, to my father, *Emanuel A. Walker*, my heartbeat that no longer beats, yet still challenges me daily. You were and are, by far, my biggest cheerleader, on and beyond this earth. May you forever be proud of the energy I put into this world. May you smile ear to ear, knowing that the lessons you instilled in me continue to nourish the world in so many ways.

This is a reminder to each of you reading this book and to those who have listened to this poem in my audiobook, *"Can We Talk? Letters & Poems to Reclaim a Bolder You,"* particularly *my clients and customers* who have trusted me on your individual and collective journeys; I appreciate you and would not be here without you. Your support, encouragement, prayers, and love mean the world to me. Thank you.

My company stands on the foundation of the two strongest pillars of change in my life - my father, last name Walker, and son, first name Walker. I stand at the forefront of our enterprise.

WALKER & WALKER
E N T E R P R I S E S

www.lolitawalker.com

I am _breath!_
As I close my eyes,
I take in the
goodness
of today &
release all negativity
from my space

www.lolitawalker.com

Copyright © 2018 - 2021 Walker & Walker Enterprises, LLC. All Rights Reserved

Affirmations are declarations to you, by you.

To purchase my 40-card deck of affirmations, inclusive of this affirmation, please visit https://www.lolitawalker.com/shop.

May each affirmation help to power your days, weeks, months, and years,

THE BONUS, PART II

QR CODE
for listening to the audio version of me speaking, *"Dear Anxiousness."*

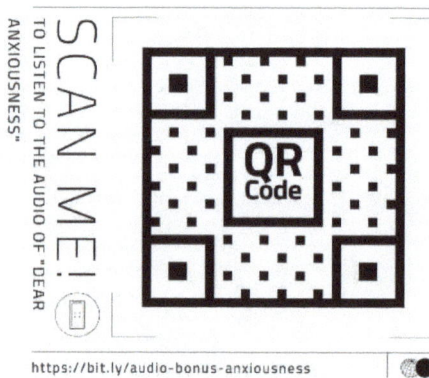

https://bit.ly/audio-bonus-anxiousness

QR CODE
for accessing books via my business website.

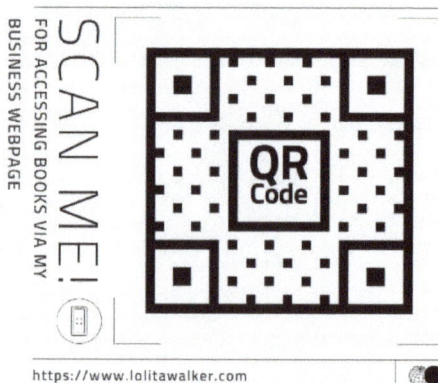

https://lolitawalker.com/

Notes & Reflections

Notes & Reflections

Notes & Reflections

Notes & Reflections

Dear Anxiousness,

Can We Talk?

WALKER & WALKER
ENTERPRISES

....

www.lolitawalker.com

2023

www.ingramcontent.com/pod-product-compliance
Lightning Source LLC
Chambersburg PA
CBHW040939100426
42812CB00015B/2627